HOMER'S

THE
ODYSSEY

A GRAPHIC NOVEL

BY DIEGO AGRIMBAU &
SMILTON ROA KLASSEN

RAINTREE
A CAPSTONE COMPANY
PUBLISHERS FOR CHILDREN

...ntree is an imprint of Capstone Global Library Limited,
a company incorporated in England and Wales having its
registered office at 264 Banbury Road, Oxford, OX2 7DY –
Registered company number: 6695582

www.raintree.co.uk
myorders@raintree.co.uk

ISBN 978 1 4747 5138 4 (paperback)
21 20 19 18 17
10 9 8 7 6 5 4 3 2 1

British Library Cataloguing in Publication Data
A full catalogue record for this book is available from the
British Library.

By Diego Agrimbau & Smilton Roa Klassen

Translated into the English language by Trusted Translations

Every effort has been made to contact copyright holders
of material reproduced in this book. Any omissions will be
rectified in subsequent printings if notice is given to the
publisher.

All the internet addresses (URLs) given in this book were
valid at the time of going to press. However, due to the
dynamic nature of the internet, some addresses may have
changed, or sites may have changed or ceased to exist since
publication. While the author and publisher regret any
inconvenience this may cause readers, no responsibility for
any such changes can be accepted by either the author or
the publisher.

Printed and bound in China.

CONTENTS

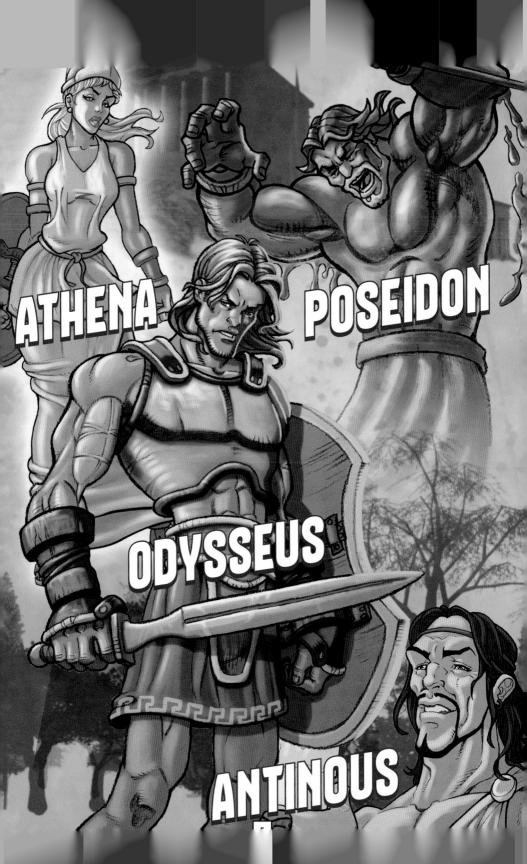

Penelope was not the only one who saw how the suitors stole the riches from the palace.

Telemachus, her son, held back his wrath in the shadows.

Are you sick of seeing these disrespectful men, Telemachus?

My name is Mentes, king of the Taphians. And I have come to give you advice.

Your father, the great Odysseus, has not died.

What do you mean, old man?!

Look for the divine Nestor in Pylos. He will tell you.

9

But there was one thing the suitors of Penelope did not know...
The young Telemachus was not travelling alone on that ship.

King Mentes was the powerful goddess Athena in disguise.

She was looking after the safety of Odysseus' son.

And she herself was the one who guided him to the old Nestor, Odysseus' companion in more than one battle during the Trojan War.

The advice of the old man was clear – Telemachus had to go to Lacedaemon, and speak with the great Menelaus, king of Sparta.

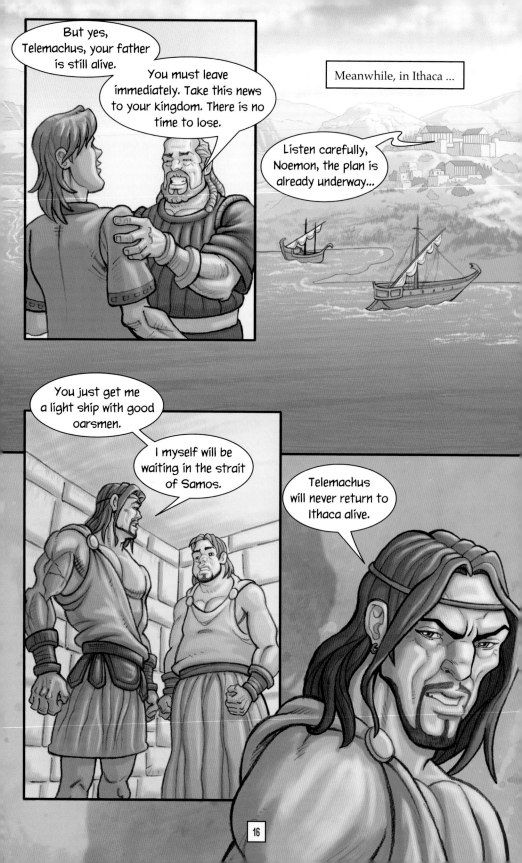

After swimming for hours, when nothing was left of that cape, Odysseus reached the mainland. His tired body needed to rest. Athena watched over him while he slept.

Odysseus did not know it yet, but he had reached Phaeacia, land of the Phaeacians.

We have finished washing all our clothes, Nausicaa. Shall we go back to the palace?

Wait, there is no rush. Let's enjoy the nice weather before going back to the city.

On the way, Odysseus was amazed at the lavish Phaeacia, one of the most green lands in the known world.

As he approached the city, his amazement increased.

The country had many riches – everything they could need. Perhaps more.

Odysseus, always clever, knew that when seeing his royal clothes, the guards of the palace would not stop him.

Odysseus told them about his land and his latest hardships, hoping to gain the trust of his hosts.

If you are the hero you say you are, then you will have no problem participating in our games. Right?

Euryalus!

It's all right, princess. I accept the challenge. If King Alcinous agrees, I will compete with his best warrior.

Odysseus did not refuse any competition. First he easily won in boxing.

Then his discus and his javelin were the ones that flew the farthest.

FISSSSSSSSSS

POW!

Only in the speed races could he not win, due to the exhaustion accumulated over the past days.

But the demonstration was done. Alcinous was more than satisfied with his guest.

"I fled with half of my men just to land in the jaws of a terrible storm."

"Then we ran aground on the island where they eat lotus, a flower that erases the memory of the one who eats it."

"Several of my men could not resist its taste."

"But the worst was yet to come..."

CHAPTER 3
THE ISLAND OF THE CYCLOPES

"After several days drifting, the dense mist covered everything. We could not see beyond our bow."

"Our ships then ran aground on a sandbank. It was an island! The drift had taken us to dry ground."

"Wild goats and sheep jumped around us with joy. But my men could only think about their delicious meat smoking before the fire."

MBEE MBEE

"We had to repair the sails, so I decided that it would be best to camp until the work was done."

SOCK SOCK

"While exploring the island, I soon found myself with a strange view."

"An enormous Cyclops was going into his home, carrying his dinner."

"The treasures and food that Cyclopes keep are legendary."

Come on, be brave. He has left, leaving the door of his cave open. It is now or never.

But, Odysseus...

What do you want that sack of wine for?

Quiet! Be stealthy.

For the beard of Poseidon! With all this we could eat for a year!

Shh! Silence! Someone is coming!

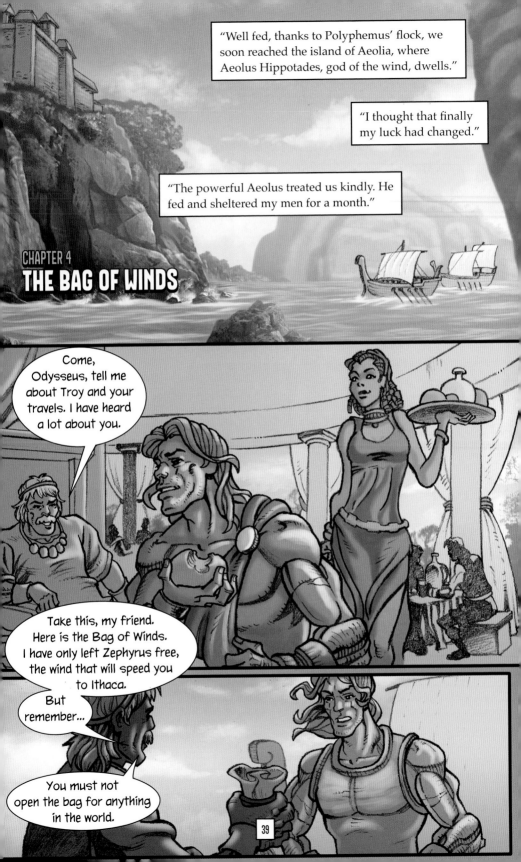

"Well fed, thanks to Polyphemus' flock, we soon reached the island of Aeolia, where Aeolus Hippotades, god of the wind, dwells."

"I thought that finally my luck had changed."

"The powerful Aeolus treated us kindly. He fed and sheltered my men for a month."

CHAPTER 4
THE BAG OF WINDS

Come, Odysseus, tell me about Troy and your travels. I have heard a lot about you.

Take this, my friend. Here is the Bag of Winds. I have only left Zephyrus free, the wind that will speed you to Ithaca.

But remember...

You must not open the bag for anything in the world.

"Those who could escape, did not get too far."

"The giants destroyed our ships by throwing rocks the size of oxen as if they were pebbles."

Oarsmen! At full speed! Let's get out of here!

"It was good fortune that helped my ship escape the thrown rocks."

"But I had lost my men, my fleet, my riches..."

"I could only pray to the gods for our luck to change."

"We sailed following Circe's directions for several days and nights."

"Until the end of the ocean opened before us."

"Once there, I followed the steps Circe had explained to me."

Bring the ram.

I will drink three cups of wine, mead and water. Then, you will sacrifice the ram.

That will be enough.

"And the first of them could not have surprised me more."

"Immediately, the souls of the underworld started to appear."

Odysseus, my son.

"That is how I discovered that my mother, Anticlea, had died."

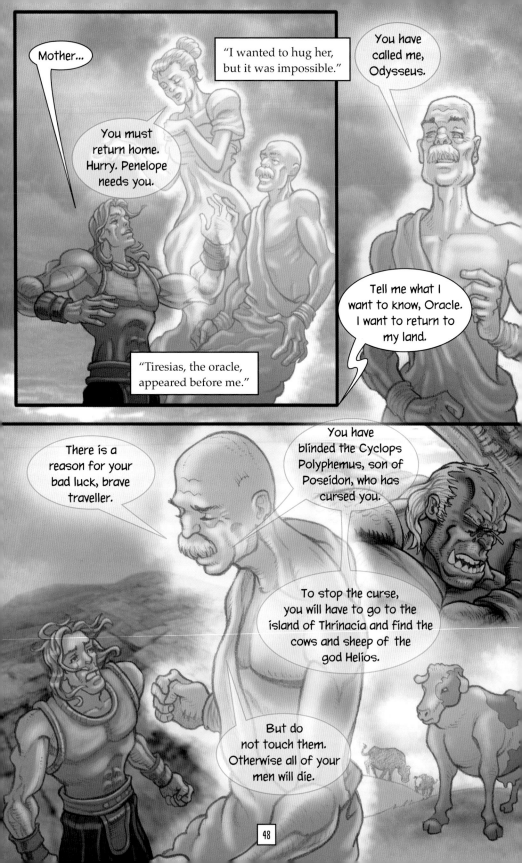

"I listened to the advice of Heracles, and soon my ship was approaching Circe's dwelling again."

I know that I have not treated you well, Odysseus. But if you could just stay...

My homeland needs me.

I understand. Penelope is a very lucky woman.

If you love me, help me return home.

CHAPTER 5
THE SIRENS' CHANT

Goodbye, Odysseus, and remember... Don't listen to the Sirens' song. That will be your downfall.

I promise I won't, beautiful Circe.

"I was lying. My curiosity was too great."

"I had to find a way to listen to that song without putting myself at risk."

Odysseus, we are already close. Are you sure about this?

Never question my plans, Eurylochus.

Have them cover their ears immediately.

Tie me up with all your strength. My life depends on how tight these ropes are. And remember...

Don't give in to my cries, dismiss my orders and threats.

"That was my plan. Bold and reckless, perhaps. But that was the only way for a mortal like me to hear their fascinating and terrifying song."

"There they were. As soon as they noticed us, they began to sing."

Come with us, divine Odysseus.

I want to go to them! Untie me! Free me!

"That is the most beautiful chant that can be heard on Earth..."

"And I am the only man who has survived hearing it."

"Six of my men died in his jaws almost immediately."

It is useless to fight! Row! Row as hard as you can!

"It took every ounce of our strength to escape."

"Finally, we reached safety."

"But because of our efforts, hunger and exhaustion overtook us."

"With my skin salted by the sea and burned by the sun, I floated for ten days and ten nights."

"When I was too tired and ready to leave to Hades, my eyes rested on something that didn't seem real."

"The current had taken me to dry land. I did not know it yet, but it was the island of the goddess Calypso."

What a beautiful mortal.

He will be my faithful companion. His heart will be mine.

You are very kind to bring a stranger into your home.

Everyone who comes to our door deserves our kindness.

This was taught to me by my king, the great Odysseus, when he still lived in these lands.

And what happened to him?

He has been unlucky with the gods. Twenty years ago he went to a war, and we never heard from him again.

His beloved Penelope insists on waiting for him, while she bears the affronts of her suitors.

But so much time has passed that...

Forget it. Finish your food and rest. Tomorrow will be another day.

At night, while the princes snored, Odysseus and his men hid their weapons.

The next day, the competition was in place.

This is the bow of my beloved husband, Odysseus. We will see who is able to tighten his rope.

Telemachus tried to save his mother, but he could not string the bow.

Then Antinous failed his attempt, like Eurymachus.

Everyone laughed when they saw the old man take the bow.

Haha! Are you sure, old man?

ABOUT THE AUTHOR

Homer is a Greek poet who lived in the 8th century BC and is credited with writing the two greatest epic poems of ancient Greece, *The Iliad* and *The Odyssey*. In his biography many traditional and legendary facts are mixed because not a lot is known about his life. In fact, there is some doubt about his historical existence. Ancient testimonies suggest he was born in the city of Chios, and one of the traditional characteristics attributed to him is blindness. In fact, his name could come from the greek phrase *Ho me horón*, which means "the one who does not see". Another theory suggests that his name may come from a society of poets called the *Homeridai*. Even today, the debate over whether his works come from an individual author or from many works combined is still discussed.

ABOUT THE RETELLING AUTHOR AND ILLUSTRATOR

Diego Agrimbau is from Buenos Aires, Argentina. He has written more than a dozen graphic novels for various publishers around the world. He has won many prizes, including the Prix Utopiales 2005 for *La Burbuja de Bertold*, First Prize Planeta DeAgostini 2009 for Comics for *Planeta Extra* and the Dibujando entre Culturas prize 2011 for *Los autómatas del Desierto*. Currently he is a contributor to the magazine *Fierro*, and writes the scripts for the comic *Los Canillitas*, published in the newspaper *Tiempo Argentino*.

Smilton Roa Klassen is an illustrator, 2D animator, cartoonist and advertising creative. He started his illustrating career making covers for the legendary publishing house Columba. He's collaborated with *Billiiken*, *Big Channel*, *Cronista Comercial*, *Compu Magazine* and other educational books. In animation, he worked for the television series *Mi familia es un dibujo*, the movies *Patoruzito I* and *II*, and the series *City Hunter* for Fox. Currently, he alternates between creating comics for the Franco-Belgian market (*Las Pelirrojas*, *La prueba Élfica*) and creating concepts, illustrations and storyboards for publicity agencies and producers.

GLOSSARY

chariot two-wheeled cart pulled by horses

cyclops mythological giant with only one eye

disrespecful lack of respect; rudeness

divine having to do with gods

foreigner person coming from another country

inhospitable unsafe, unwelcoming

lavish has or produces something in large amounts

legendary fame given to a person for accomplishing great things; someone who is legendary is the best at what he or she does

mercy when someone gives lighter punishment or treatment to a person who deserves more

mortal human; a being who will eventually die

oracle place or person that a god speaks through; in myths, gods used oracles to predict the future or to tell people how to solve problems

pity feeling of sympathy for the hardships of another

sacrifice offer something to a god

shipwreck destruction of a ship at sea

suitor man who is trying to persuade a woman to marry him

wrath great anger

AN UNFORGETTABLE JOURNEY

The Odyssey, along with *The Iliad*, is a great Greek epic poem. It has 24 parts, which tell the unforgettable journey of the return of Odysseus to his kingdom in Ithaca after the end of the Trojan War. Odysseus is characterized by his intelligence and wisdom, thanks to which, according to the legend, the Greeks were able to end the nine-year war. In the story, Odysseus comes up with the famous plan of the Trojan Horse when he realizes that the walls of the city can't be climbed.

Penelope, wife of Odysseus and queen of Ithaca, was no less clever than her husband. Thanks to a ploy, for ten years she managed to avoid marrying one of her many suitors. She had promised to choose a new husband when she finished her weaving (as can be seen on page 7 of the story). But what nobody knew was that during the night, Penelope undid the work she had done during the day, so that her weaving would not be completed until Odysseus returned.

Each of the creatures that Odysseus crosses paths with throughout his journey has its own history, and they appear in other books, both ancient and modern. One of these characters is the great Cyclops Polyphemus, son of Poseidon, and the nymph Thoosa. It is because of the damage that Odysseus has caused Polyphemus that Poseidon wrecks his boat when Odysseus leaves the island of Calypso. Polyphemus was not only a terrible monster in this story. He also appears in a love story from ancient Greece. It is the *Fable of Acis and Galatea*. According to this story, Polyphemus was hopelessly in love with a sea nymph, Galatea, but she did not feel the same way. One afternoon, upon learning that Galatea loved a handsome shepherd named Acis, Polyphemus fell into an uncontrollable anger that led him to kill the shepherd. The story ends with Galatea changing the soul of Acis into a river.

Other famous creatures with which Odysseus crosses paths are the Sirens. But as you can see in the pictures, these particular sirens are not the classic romantic and friendly creatures found in fairy tales. In *The Odyssey,* they are hybrid creatures that are traditionally half woman, half animal, but in this case, instead of a fish tail they have bird legs. The sirens were a terrible threat for mythological sailors. Their song steered them towards rocks where the ships ran aground, at which point they ate the crew.

Throughout the history of literature, many tales have used the story of Odysseus. In ancient Roman literature, *The Aeneid* progresses much like *The Odyssey.* It tells the journey of Aeneas, the only Trojan prince who survived the Trojan War. He goes from the shores of Troy to the region of Lazio, where his descendants, Romulus and Remus, would found Rome. In the 20th century, the Irish novelist James Joyce rewrote a contemporary version of Odysseus' journey in his novel *Ulysses* (which was Odysseus' name in Roman mythology).

DISCUSSION
QUESTIONS

1. What do you think was more important for Odysseus, his strength or his intelligence? Use examples from the text to support your answer.

2. What other trick could Penelope have done to avoid marrying one of her suitors?

3. Why do you think Odysseus risked listening to the song of the Sirens? Did it seem like a wise decision or was it very dangerous?

4. Do you agree with how Odysseus dealt with the suitors? What else could he have done?

WRITING
PROMPTS

1. Odysseus made Polyphemus fall asleep with wine. Then he attacked the Cyclops with a stake to help him and his men escape. Can you think of any other plan that could have got him out of the cave? Write down your plan.

2. Pretend you are Odysseus while he was trapped on the island of Calypso. Write a letter home to Penelope.

3. What might have happened on Telemachus' journey back to Ithaca after Athena told him the truth about Odysseus? Write about any of the adventures he could have had.

4. Imagine you are part of the crew on Odysseus' ship. Write about a day on board and what kind of wonders you would see in the ocean.

THE ODYSSEY AND FILM

The Odyssey is a story that has fascinated many audiences. Since the very beginning of film, the adventures of Odysseus have been a source of inspiration. In 1905, the pioneer of adventure films, Georges Melies, made a short film about Odysseus' encounter with Polyphemus in his cave. He titled it *Ulysses and the Giant Polyphemus*. The film only lasts four minutes, but the special effects achieved within its scenes dazzled audiences at the time.

In 1954, the famous American actor Kirk Douglas starred as *Ulysses*. It was an Italian production that was filmed in the same places where Homer set his poem.

In 1997, an adaptation for television called *The Odyssey* was made in the form of a miniseries. In this recreation the famous Italian film star Isabella Rossellini played the goddess Athena and British actor Christopher Lee played Tiresias. The film was a success. It won an Emmy and was nominated for a Golden Globe.

In 2000, the film *O Brother Where Art Thou?*, by the Cohen brothers, took Odysseus' journey but set the story in the southern United States during the 1930s. In this film, Homer appears in the credits as one of the authors.

READ THEM ALL!

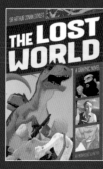

SIR ARTHUR CONAN DOYLE'S
THE LOST WORLD
A GRAPHIC NOVEL

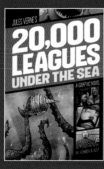

JULES VERNE'S
20,000 LEAGUES UNDER THE SEA
A GRAPHIC NOVEL

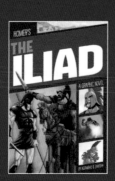

HOMER'S
THE ILIAD
A GRAPHIC NOVEL

HERMAN MELVILLE'S
MOBY DICK
A GRAPHIC NOVEL

ROBIN HOOD
A GRAPHIC NOVEL

ARTHUR CONAN DOYLE'S
THE HOUND OF THE BASKERVILLES
A GRAPHIC NOVEL

MARY SHELLEY'S
FRANKENSTEIN
A GRAPHIC NOVEL

ROBERT LOUIS STEVENSON'S
TREASURE ISLAND
A GRAPHIC NOVEL

CHARLES DICKENS'S
A CHRISTMAS CAROL
A GRAPHIC NOVEL

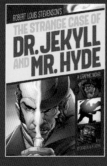

ROBERT LOUIS STEVENSON'S
THE STRANGE CASE OF DR. JEKYLL AND MR. HYDE
A GRAPHIC NOVEL

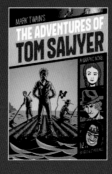

MARK TWAIN'S
THE ADVENTURES OF TOM SAWYER
A GRAPHIC NOVEL

DRACULA

JULES VERNE'S
AROUND THE WORLD IN 80 DAYS
A GRAPHIC NOVEL

DANIEL DEFOE'S
ROBINSON CRUSOE
A GRAPHIC NOVEL

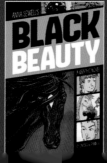

ANNA SEWELL'S
BLACK BEAUTY
A GRAPHIC NOVEL

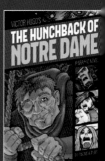

VICTOR HUGO'S
THE HUNCHBACK OF NOTRE DAME
A GRAPHIC NOVEL

JOHANN DAVID WYSS
THE SWISS FAMILY ROBINSON
A GRAPHIC NOVEL

H. G. WELLS'S
THE WAR OF THE WORLDS
A GRAPHIC NOVEL

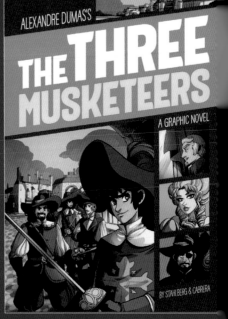

ALEXANDRE DUMAS'S
THE THREE MUSKETEERS
A GRAPHIC NOVEL

BY STAHLBERG & CABRERA

PERSEUS AND MEDUSA
A GRAPHIC NOVEL

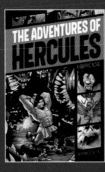

THE ADVENTURES OF HERCULES
A GRAPHIC NOVEL

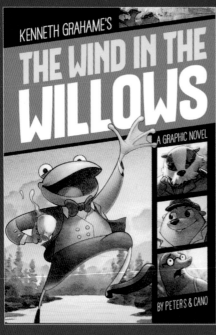

KENNETH GRAHAME'S
THE WIND IN THE WILLOWS
A GRAPHIC NOVEL

BY PETERS & CANO

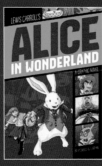

LEWIS CARROLL'S
ALICE IN WONDERLAND
A GRAPHIC NOVEL

JONATHAN SWIFT'S
GULLIVER'S TRAVELS
A GRAPHIC NOVEL

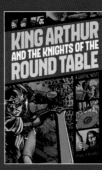

KING ARTHUR AND THE KNIGHTS OF THE ROUND TABLE
A GRAPHIC NOVEL

J.M. BARRIE'S
PETER PAN
A GRAPHIC NOVEL

BY HOENA & CANO

ONLY FROM RAINTREE BOOKS!